THE ESSENTIAL MEANS OF GRACE

THE ESSENTIAL MEANS OF GRACE

Paul Washer

Reformation Heritage Books
Grand Rapids, Michigan

The Essential Means of Grace

Reformation Heritage Books
3070 29th St. SE
Grand Rapids, MI 49512
616-977-0889
orders@heritagebooks.org
www.heritagebooks.org

Printed in the United States of America
22 23 24 25 26 27/10 9 8 7 6 5 4 3 2

Library of Congress Cataloging-in-Publication Data

Names: Washer, Paul, 1961- author.
Title: The essential means of grace / Paul Washer.
Description: Grand Rapids, Michigan : Reformation Heritage Books, 2020. | Includes bibliographical references.
Identifiers: LCCN 2020019104 (print) | LCCN 2020019105 (ebook) | ISBN 9781601788078 (paperback) | ISBN 9781601788085 (epub)
Subjects: LCSH: Grace (Theology) | Spiritual formation.
Classification: LCC BT761.3 .W37 2020 (print) | LCC BT761.3 (ebook) | DDC 234—dc23
LC record available at https://lccn.loc.gov/2020019104
LC ebook record available at https://lccn.loc.gov/2020019105

For additional Reformed literature, request a free book list from Reformation Heritage Books at the above regular or email address.

Contents

1

The Means of Grace

Do you lament your lack of spiritual growth? Do you long to be more conformed to the image of Christ? If you answered in the affirmative, then this brief work is for you. However, you must be forewarned that you will find no easy answer or quick fix to your spiritual life in these pages, nor will you discover something novel or new. Here you will find only an ancient remedy to an ancient problem. A hard medicine will be offered to you that most people would rather bypass for a more pleasant elixir. However, if you are sick of being sick, if you have wandered long enough in the foothills and are willing to take the hard path up the mountain, then this little work may offer you some help—some means of growing beyond where you are!

There is a very important theological phrase in Latin that every Christian of every language ought to learn and apply to his or her life. The phrase is *media gratiae,* and its English translation is *means of grace*. For centuries the church has employed this little phrase to describe those means or gifts that the Lord Jesus Christ has given to the church for its ongoing sanctification or growth in holiness.

The most prominent and essential of these means are the study of the Scriptures, devotion to prayer, and participation in the life and ministry of the local church. These means are *not works* that must be accomplished in order to earn or merit salvation, but they are gifts from God through which the believer may grow in the salvation that he or she has received by grace alone through faith alone in Jesus Christ. As the apostle Paul wrote, "For by grace you have been saved through faith, and that not of yourselves; it is the gift of God, not of works, lest anyone should boast" (Eph. 2:8–9).

The Scriptures prove over and over that salvation is *monergistic*—that is, the work of one. God is the author and agent of our salvation and we are the objects of His saving work. However, with equal force the Scriptures also teach that our growth in sanctification is *synergistic*—that is, the collective work of two or more. This is wonderfully illustrated in Paul's admonition to the church in Philippi: "Therefore, my beloved, as you have always obeyed, not as in my presence only, but now much more in my absence, work out your own salvation with fear and trembling; for it is God who works in you both to will and to do for His good pleasure" (Phil. 2:12–13).

Take note of the perfect balance. Since it is God who works in us both to will and to do for His good pleasure, we are to work out our own salvation with fear and trembling—that is, with the greatest reverence toward God and the most profound solemnity with regard to the task. There is no room in biblical Christianity for apathy, a lack of discipline, or a "let go and let God" attitude.

To more fully understand what is meant by the phrase *media gratiae*, it is helpful to add the Latin adjective *ordinarius*, or ordinary. *Media gratiae* refers to the ordinary means of grace or the ordinary way in which God has decreed that Christians will grow in conformity to Christ. We live in a day when it seems that everyone in the church is waiting for something extraordinary—a move of the Spirit that will correct all our spiritual maladies in a moment's time and with little effort or cost on our part. Although such an extraordinary revival is altogether possible and should be desired, it is not God's ordinary means of growing His church. Our desire for the extraordinary should never lead us to neglect the ordinary means that God has given us to grow. In fact, in God's economy He usually does not perform the extraordinary until His people have exhausted the ordinary means that He has provided.

Having stated the above, it is highly unlikely that the contemporary church or the individual Christian has exhausted the ordinary means of grace—that we have learned all that the Scriptures have to say, that we have emptied all of God's promises in prayer, that our intimacy with the Father, Son, and Holy Spirit has no more room to grow, or that we have reaped every benefit that is to be gained from fellowship with a local church. Is it not more likely that we have been derelict or at least careless, even slothful, with these ordinary but essential means of grace? We must be careful that we do not despise the day of small things (Zech. 4:10). In fact, Jesus taught, "Take heed what you hear. With the same measure you use, it will be measured to you; and to you who hear, more will be given" (Mark 4:24). And again, "He who is faithful in what is least is faithful also in much" (Luke 16:10). The believer who neglects the ordinary will rarely ever witness the extraordinary!

Although the phrase *media gratiae* is for the most part unknown among modern evangelicals, it is only because we are ignorant of many of the historical truths of biblical Christianity that once served to strengthen and purify Christ's church. There was a time when the phrase *media gratiae* or "means of grace" was a part of every Christian's vocabulary. This is proven by question 88 in the Westminster Shorter Catechism that was used to teach children and new converts about the basics of Christianity:

> *Question:* What are the outward means whereby Christ communicates to us the benefits of redemption?
>
> *Answer:* The outward and ordinary means whereby Christ communicates to us the benefits of redemption are, His ordinances, especially the word, sacraments, and prayer;[1] all of which are made effectual to the elect for salvation.[2]

1. "Go therefore and make disciples of all the nations, baptizing them in the name of the Father and of the Son and of the Holy Spirit, teaching them to observe all things that I have commanded you; and lo, I am with you always, even to the end of the age. Amen." (Matt. 28:19–20).

2. "Then those who gladly received his word were baptized; and that day about three thousand souls were added to them. And they continued steadfastly in the apostles' doctrine and fellowship, in the breaking of bread, and in prayers.... So continuing daily with one accord in the temple, and breaking bread from house to house, they ate their food with gladness and simplicity of heart, praising God and having favor with all the people. And the Lord added to the church daily those who were being saved" (Acts 2:41–42, 46–47).

It is important to note that giving emphasis or even priority to the "means of grace" was not confined to Presbyterian or strictly Reformed churches, but was widely taught by early Baptists and other evangelicals. Question 95 of the Baptist Catechism, written by the well-known Particular Baptist, Benjamin Keach (1640–1704), follows word for word the Westminster Shorter Catechism's definition of the means of grace.

We live in an age when too many sincere believers rely upon internet preachers, blogs, tweets, and sound bites. Although some of this may be useful, nothing will replace the simple but efficient means that the Lord Himself has given His people to grow. We must turn our feet toward the ancient paths[3] of the Scriptures and the paths of those faithful men and women who have gone before us. In the pages to come, we will briefly consider the three ordinary means of grace that God has graciously bestowed upon the individual Christian and the church at large to promote the godliness that finds its desire in greater conformity to the image of Christ: the Scriptures, prayer, and the ministry and ordinances of the local church.

---

3. "Thus says the LORD: 'Stand in the ways and see, and ask for the old paths, where the good way *is*, and walk in it; then you will find rest for your souls'" (Jer. 6:16).

Chapter Questions and Reflections

1. What is the meaning of the Latin phrase *media gratiae*?

2. Identify the means of grace that are listed in this chapter.

3. Why are the means of grace often referred to as *ordinary* means of grace?

4. What are the dangers of neglecting the ordinary while we wait for the extraordinary?

5. Explain the meaning and implications of question 88 in the Westminster Shorter Catechism.

2

The Scriptures

After our brief introduction to the means of grace we will now consider the first and foremost—the study and exposition of the Scriptures. Apart from the triune God Himself, the greatest and most indispensable gift that the Lord has given to the church is the Bible. There is no other source of inerrant truth regarding God's person, decrees, works, will, and promises. The apostle Paul in his letter to his young co-laborer, Timothy, powerfully affirms this truth: "All Scripture is given by inspiration of God, and is profitable for doctrine, for reproof, for correction, for instruction in righteousness, that the man of God may be complete, thoroughly equipped for every good work" (2 Tim. 3:16–17).

Although the Scriptures have no need of human validation, for our sakes it is important to affirm that the inspiration, inerrancy, and absolute essentiality of the Scriptures have been the abiding conviction of the true church down through the ages. The Westminster Confession and the 1689 London Baptist Confession declare:

> The Holy Scriptures are the only sufficient, certain, and infallible standard of all saving knowledge,

> faith, and obedience.... To preserve and propagate the truth better and to establish and comfort the church with greater certainty against the corruption of the flesh and the malice of Satan and the world, the Lord put this revelation completely in writing. Therefore, the Holy Scriptures are absolutely necessary, because God's former ways of revealing his will to his people have now ceased.[1]

If we hesitate to any degree in affirming the inspiration, inerrancy, or sufficiency of the Scriptures, then a sure foundation for the Christian life will always remain beyond our reach. We will be "tossed to and fro and carried about with every wind of doctrine" (Eph. 4:14). We will be enslaved to our frequent and erroneous thoughts, emotions, and impulses. We will be plagued with an ever-fluctuating hope, an unpredictable temperament, and an erratic conduct.

The Study of Scripture

During His temptation in the wilderness, Jesus affirmed the absolute essentiality of the Scriptures in the life of the believer when He declared, "It is written, 'Man shall not live by bread alone, but by every word that proceeds from the mouth of God'" (Matt. 4:4). Here we see that we must feed upon the Word for spiritual nutrition with the greatest diligence as we feed upon physical food for our daily nourishment. The Bible is an inspired book, but it is not a magical book. Its words and truths will not simply fly off

1. *The 1689 Baptist Confession in Modern English* (Cape Coral, Fla.: Founders Press, 2017), 1.1. Cf. Westminster Confession of Faith 1.1.

the pages into the heart and mind of its possessor. To gain benefit from the Scriptures we must study the Scriptures, and that with diligence. The apostle Paul wrote to Timothy, "Be diligent to present yourself approved to God, as a worker who does not need to be ashamed, rightly dividing the word of truth" (2 Tim. 2:15). And again, "Till I come, give attention to reading, to exhortation, to doctrine.... Meditate on these things; give yourself entirely to them, that your progress may be evident to all" (1 Tim. 4:13–15).

Although it is true that Paul was exhorting a man who had been ordained for the ministry, his exhortations have a wider and more general application to every believer. A biblical, Reformed, and evangelical faith calls upon every believer—the most mature saint and the most recent convert—to study, understand, and apply the Scriptures. When Jesus declared, "Man shall not live by bread alone, but by every word that proceeds from the mouth of God," He most certainly had in mind every man (Matt. 4:4). How much more those of the household of faith!

If you are not convinced and committed to study the Scriptures personally, diligently, and consistently, then very little of what is written in the rest of this book will benefit you. Our journey to Christian maturity is founded upon our knowledge of the person, decrees, works, will, and promises of God. Such knowledge is impossible apart from a diligent personal study of the Scriptures, consistent exposure to biblical exposition, and fellowship in a truly biblical church. If we neglect this foundation, we have little hope of advancing in the knowledge of God or growing in conformity to His will.

Whether you are new to the Christian faith or are a saint of many years, the greatest means of growing in the knowledge of God is the simple reading of the Scriptures from Genesis to Revelation over and over again as a daily *life discipline.* As an ordained minister, I study the Bible for hours a day, and yet I have discovered that nothing replaces the simple daily reading of the Scriptures. Therefore, I recommend to you what has been of the greatest benefit to me. Set aside a time each day simply to read through the Scriptures. Do not hurry or fret about a slow pace. Some portions of Scripture allow for a more rapid reading than others. Some days you may read through three to five chapters. Other days, you may read only one. The goal is to enjoy the Scriptures, to grow in the knowledge of God, and to be transformed by that knowledge. For your daily reading, I heartily recommend a study Bible for quick reference. It will help you navigate through difficult terms and phrases and keep you between the lines of historic, evangelical Christianity. The four study Bibles that I have found most helpful are the *Reformation Heritage Study Bible,* the *Reformation Study Bible,* the *ESV Study Bible,* and the *MacArthur Study Bible.*[2]

As you read through the Scriptures, you will undoubtedly discover many key or foundational texts regarding great theological truths and other texts that

2. *The Reformation Heritage KJV Study Bible,* ed. Joel R. Beeke, Michael Barrett, Gerald Bilkes, and Paul Smalley (Grand Rapids: Reformation Heritage Books, 2014); *The Reformation Study Bible,* ed. R. C. Sproul (Orlando, Fla.: Reformation Trust, 2015); *ESV Study Bible* (Wheaton, Ill.: Crossway, 2011); *MacArthur Study Bible,* ed. John MacArthur (Nashville, Tenn.: Thomas Nelson, 2013).

will have special significance for your current personal circumstance and need. These should be put to memory. Although there are many methods used to memorize Scripture, all have one common denominator—hard work and persistence! We often think that other Christians excel in specific disciplines simply because of their gifts, talents, or personalities. They excel because it is easier for them than for us. However, for the most part, I have found this to be untrue. Although some may possess a keener mind for Scripture memory than others, they excel because they have recognized the great benefit of internalizing the Scriptures and they are willing to do the work. The psalmist wrote, "Your word I have hidden in my heart, that I might not sin against You" (Ps. 119:11). The inverse is, "Your word I have *not* hidden in my heart, that I *might* sin against You."

I am aware that my recommendation may sound overly simplistic to many. However, reading the Scriptures from cover to cover and over and over again was the coveted practice of most of the greatest saints in church history, and it remains so today. If you are at a loss as to how to begin, it may be helpful to obtain Robert Murray M'Cheyne's Bible reading calendar.[3] For several decades, it has been a great help to many saints who have committed themselves to the reading of the Scriptures.

---

3. R. M. M'Cheyne (1813–1843) was the minister of St. Peter's Church, Dundee, Scotland. He devised a Bible reading calendar that guides the believer through the Old Testament once and the New Testament and Psalms twice in a calendar year. It is available in print and online.

The Exposition of Scripture

In conjunction with our personal reading and study of the Scriptures is the teaching and preaching of the Scriptures in the context of the local church by the faithful elders who shepherd us. To sit under godly pastors who are devoted to the study of the Scriptures, live the Scriptures, and proclaim the Scriptures is a great means of grace for the people of God. This kind of minister is wonderfully exemplified in the life and ministry of Ezra, of whom the Scriptures testify, "For Ezra had prepared his heart to seek the Law of the LORD, and to do it, and to teach statutes and ordinances in Israel" (Ezra 7:10). It is further exemplified by the ideal Levitical priest described in the book of Malachi: "The law of truth was in his mouth, and injustice was not found on his lips. He walked with Me in peace and equity, and turned many away from iniquity. For the lips of a priest should keep knowledge, and people should seek the law from his mouth; for he is the messenger of the LORD of hosts" (Mal. 2:6–7).

As nothing can replace our personal study of the Scriptures, so nothing can replace the ministry of a godly pastor expounding the Scriptures to the flock he personally knows, loves, and serves sacrificially. In recent years, the growth of the internet has allowed believers access to some of the most capable preachers in the world, but this has been a mixed blessing. Accessing an internet ministry is no substitute for being a vital member of a local congregation, and the greatest internet preachers, though beneficial, are no substitute for a godly pastor who is faithful to the Scriptures. He may not possess academic credentials or extraordinary gifts, but if he is a faithful pastor, he is worth more to your sanctification than all the internet preachers combined! To neglect this great means of grace is a mark of spiritual immaturity and dullness of heart.

It is also important to remember that even the greatest preachers are mere men who are capable of error and must be judged by the Word of God. Like the Bereans of Paul's day, we are to receive "the word with all readiness" and yet search "the Scriptures daily to find out whether these things were so" (Acts 17:11). We must "not despise prophetic utterances" (that is, biblical preaching), but we must "examine everything carefully."[4] For these admonitions to be obeyed, we must study the word of God personally, diligently, and consistently.

Before I go further, I must give a brief admonition to pastors. You are the most privileged men on the planet and a great stewardship has been laid upon you. If the believer is called upon to work out his or her salvation in fear and trembling, how much more must you fulfill your ministry with an even greater degree of solemnity (Phil. 2:12). Do you not realize that the most common complaint of the believer in the pew is that their pastors seem more concerned with programs and strategies and the number of their flock than with the study of God's Word, secret

4. The gift of prophecy has ceased. However, the admonition has continued relevancy for the church. The words of the prophets are permanently recorded in the inerrant words of the Scriptures. We should not despise the accurate exposition and application of these prophetic words even when they expose, rebuke, correct, and admonish us. However, we must examine all proclamation in the light of the Scriptures to ensure that it is accurate and edifying (see 1 Thess. 5:20–21, NASB).

prayer, modeling a godly life, and the exposition of Scripture? Dear brothers, let this not be said of us. Let us be like Ezra of old who "prepared his heart to seek the Law of the LORD, and to do it, and to teach statutes and ordinances in Israel" (Ezra 7:10). Like the apostle let us say to every distraction, "but we will give ourselves continually to prayer and to the ministry of the word" (Acts 6:4).

The Use of Scripture in Worship

The Scriptures are not only to be studied personally and expounded through preaching, but they are to be communicated in and through our public worship. This is accomplished through three primary venues—the public reading of the Scriptures, public exposition of the Scriptures, and singing of the Scriptures.

The public reading of lengthy portions of the Scriptures is a rarity today. In fact, most would be surprised to know that it was considered a central part of congregational worship by early Reformed and evangelical churches. This view was not founded upon the personal preferences of our spiritual forefathers, but is actually commanded in the Scriptures. In 1 Timothy 3:15, the apostle Paul gives lengthy instruction regarding "how [one] ought to conduct [himself] in the household of God"; he commanded that the reading of the Scriptures be a central part of congregational worship: "Till I come, give attention to reading, to exhortation, to doctrine" (1 Tim. 4:13).

We build our house on the sand when we ignore this command on the grounds that it "slows down" the service or because modern man has lost his ability to listen with attentiveness. We must not acquiesce or conform to the low standards of our culture. One of the countless errors and heresies of Roman Catholicism is that it conformed Christianity to culture in order to make it more appealing and acceptable. In contrast, the Reformers remained faithful to the Scriptures and called the surrounding cultures to conform to its high standard. Roman Catholicism only lowered and polluted Christianity, but the Reformed faith raised cultures to new spiritual, academic, economic, and social heights. We must not tolerate the notion that the people of this internet age of sound bites can no longer bear lengthy readings of Scripture or sermons that go beyond twenty minutes. Instead, we must lovingly and patiently read the Scriptures until the people are transformed by them.

Walking hand in hand with the reading of the Scriptures is the faithful exposition of Scripture by godly elders, teachers, and evangelists who are devoted to its study. This is also a form of worship in that the one proclaiming is declaring, expounding, and extolling the attributes and works of God. In turn, this generates in the heart of the believing congregation a greater reverence, esteem, and love for God. The great Geneva Reformer John Calvin once wrote, "It ought always to be the aim of a good teacher, to turn away the eyes of men from the world, that they may look up to heaven."[5] True biblical preaching is not primarily about the communication of life principles so that the congregation might navigate its way to its "best life now." It is about the communication of the knowledge of God resulting in faith, worship, and

5. *Calvin's Commentaries*, on Titus 1:2, 21:283.

heart-felt obedience. Like the public reading of Scripture, this historical view of preaching is now a rarity, and yet it remains an essential means of grace. As a Christian you must make this a top priority. No matter what the cost or whatever hardship you must endure, seek out fellowship in a church whose elders and teachers are devoted to the study of Scripture, who consider preaching and teaching to be *the* ministry of their lives, and whose sermons provide you with the knowledge and motivation to worship God in spirit and in truth, "for the Father is seeking such to worship Him" (John 4:23).

Finally, walking hand in hand with both the reading of Scripture and its exposition is the singing of Scripture. Congregational singing is an act of worship, which is to be directed exclusively to God, with the residual result of edifying the congregation. For such singing to be pleasing to God and edifying for the saints it must be both biblical and didactic.[6] Some Reformed churches teach that it is safest and best to limit singing in the churches to God's original canonical manual for singing, namely the Psalms, while other Reformed churches feel comfortable singing hymns that convey the great doctrinal truths, admonitions, encouragements, and warnings of the Scriptures. Though strong views are held on both sides of this

6. The word "didactic" is derived from the Greek verb *didaskein*, which means "to teach." Worship songs that are didactic are instructive, informational, or educational. They communicate biblical truth. The fact that singing must be didactic is proved by Paul's words to the Colossians, "Let the word of Christ dwell in you richly in all wisdom, teaching and admonishing one another in psalms and hymns and spiritual songs, singing with grace in your hearts to the Lord" (3:16).

issue, both views agree that singing in corporate worship is a valid and important means of grace for God's people. Many scholars and church historians have argued that the great truths of the Reformation were not only communicated to the common people through the preaching of the Reformers, but also through the biblical hymns that were written and sung by the church. It is not coincidental that the hymnal or songbook of the Scriptures—the book of Psalms—is also a primary resource for the study of many of the greatest doctrines of Christianity, especially with regard to the doctrine of God. The apostle Paul in his letter to the Colossians also affirms this relationship between worship and the word: "Let the word of Christ dwell in you richly in all wisdom, teaching and admonishing one another in psalms and hymns and spiritual songs, singing with grace in your hearts to the Lord" (Col. 3:16).

Biblical emotions are a pleasant gift from God, and biblical worship certainly has the power to move the emotions in a manner that is conformed to the will of God. However, our emotional response to the music, rhythm, or lyrics of a hymn or chorus is no indication of its propriety. It must be tested by the Scriptures and it must communicate the great truths of the Scriptures. It is not enough for the hymn to be void of heresy, but it must also be replete with truth! When the music is silenced, and the rhythm fades, it will be the truth of the Scriptures communicated through the hymn that remains.

The Great Theme of Scripture

We have established that the Scriptures are the great means through which we are not only saved,[7] but also sanctified. However, we would be remiss if we did not set forth a most essential truth—that the central theme of Scripture is the person and redemptive work of the Lord Jesus Christ. He is the lodestone of the Scriptures and must be at the beginning, center, and end of all our reading, study, memorization, meditation, preaching, and singing.

Although the gospel message falls under the category of the Scriptures, it is such an important and exquisite theme that it must be treated separately. Many preachers down through the ages have affirmed that the dust of the Bible is gold, that the smallest jot and tittle of Scripture is more valuable than all the other books that have been and will be written. Nevertheless, even in the Scriptures there is the one message, the one truth that stands above them all—"that Christ died for our sins according to the Scriptures, and that He was buried, and that He rose again the third day according to the Scriptures" (1 Cor. 15:3–4). In these few affirmations are found the greatest revelation of God and the whole of our salvation.

The gospel is not only "the power of God to salvation for everyone who believes," but it is also the greatest catalyst or incitement for our advance and perseverance in the faith (Rom. 1:16). The apostle Paul wrote: "For the love

7. "From childhood you have known the Holy Scriptures, which are able to make you wise for salvation through faith which is in Christ Jesus" (2 Tim. 3:15).

of Christ compels us, because we judge thus: that if One died for all, then all died; and He died for all, that those who live should live no longer for themselves, but for Him who died for them and rose again" (2 Cor. 5:14–15).

In the gospel of Jesus Christ is found every reason for faith and every incentive for growth, endurance, service, and sacrifice. One glimpse of Christ is enough to propel a regenerate heart through ten thousand lifetimes of spiritual warfare, battles with the flesh, inward trials, persecutions, and physical debilitations. It was a far-off glimpse of Christ in the gospel that moved Moses to forsake Egypt and the passing pleasures of sin, to suffer affliction with the people of God, and to make a stand against the most powerful ruler on earth.[8] It was a glimpse of Christ that moved Paul to give himself to a life of tireless service and martyrdom. It was a glimpse of Christ that empowered John Bunyan to spend years behind bars rather than deny his call to preach the gospel. It was a glimpse of Christ that sent William Carey to India, Hudson Taylor to China, and George Müller to the orphans of Bristol. Borrowing from the writer of Hebrews (11:32), "And what more shall I say? For the time would fail me to tell of" the countless saints throughout the ages who did and endured extraordinary things because of one

---

8. "By faith Moses, when he became of age, refused to be called the son of Pharaoh's daughter, choosing rather to suffer affliction with the people of God than to enjoy the passing pleasures of sin, esteeming the reproach of Christ greater riches than the treasures in Egypt; for he looked to the reward. By faith he forsook Egypt, not fearing the wrath of the king; for he endured as seeing Him who is invisible" (Heb. 11:24–27).

singular motivation—that Christ died for sinners! If you want to join this esteemed group in similar exploits and endurance, then above all seek Christ in the Scriptures and prayer. What the wise man said of wisdom finds its ultimate fulfillment in Christ—He is more precious than jewels; and nothing you desire compares with Him![9]

Chapter Questions and Reflections

1. What is the "foremost" means of grace that God has given to the believer? Why should it be considered foremost or foundational?

2. What Bible text proves the absolute essentiality of the Scriptures? What truth does it communicate?

3. Do you agree with the following statement? Why? "If we hesitate to any degree in affirming the inspiration, inerrancy, or sufficiency of the Scriptures, then a sure foundation for the Christian life will always remain beyond our reach."

4. What does the following statement mean? Do you agree? "The Bible is an inspired book, but it is not a magical book. Its words and truths will not simply fly off the pages into the heart and mind of its possessor. To gain benefit from the

9. "She is more precious than rubies, and all the things you may desire cannot compare with her" (Prov. 3:15).

Scriptures we must study the Scriptures, and that with diligence."

5. How should we study the Scriptures? What study tool does this chapter suggest? Why?

6. According to this chapter, how important is it that we unite with a local church and sit under the expository preaching of qualified elders?

7. What are the three primary venues through which the Scriptures are communicated in and through our public worship? What is the meaning of each?

8. Why should the gospel of Jesus Christ be the great focus of all our study, preaching, and worship? Explain why Christ and His gospel is the greatest incentive in the Christian life.

3

Prayer

Both daily Bible reading and prayer seem to battle it out for the title for the most neglected discipline in the Christian life. At the risk of sounding simplistic, this neglect is the source of nearly all the spiritual maladies that afflict the individual believer and the church collectively. Everyone seems to be unanimous regarding the necessity of the Word and prayer, and equally unanimous in admitting personal neglect of both. It has often been said by both ministers and laity, "I have never known of a dying believer who lamented that they had spent *too* much time in the Word of God and prayer."

All of this must lead us to a very important but painful question, "Why do we find prayer so difficult?" The most obvious reason is our flesh and its stubborn self-sufficiency. Our flesh hates secret prayer because it is a denial of self-sufficiency, does not allow for self-glory, and turns the admiration and applause of men from us to God. In one sense, our flesh can be a guide to what is truly important in the Christian life—that which the flesh most opposes is that which is most essential. And what does our flesh oppose more than the reading of Scripture and private prayer?

Another reason for our struggles with prayer is our simple lack of faith. Prayer is an opportunity to participate in the miraculous and to behold God as He does "exceedingly abundantly above all that we ask or think" (Eph. 3:20). In Luke 18:1–8, Jesus gives one of His greatest discourses regarding the willingness of God to respond to persevering prayer. He then ends with one of the saddest commentaries on His people's lack of faith and devotion to prayer: "Nevertheless, when the Son of Man comes, will He really find faith on the earth?" (Luke 18:8).

Dear brothers and sisters in Christ, let this not be a description of our generation. Let us not be among those who have not because they ask not (James 4:2). Let us put away the arm of the flesh and its feeble resources and give ourselves wholly and persistently to God in prayer. Did He not promise, "For the eyes of the Lord run to and fro throughout the whole earth, to show Himself strong on behalf of those whose heart is loyal to Him" (2 Chron. 16:9)? And again, "You who make mention of the Lord, do not keep silent, and give Him no rest till He establishes and till He makes Jerusalem a praise in the earth" (Isa. 62:6–7). The less we trust in the flesh and the more we throw ourselves upon God in prayer, the more we will see His miraculous power working in us and through us. With promises like these how can we despair? How can we not rise up and go forward?

Following Christ's Example

To expose the senselessness of our self-sufficiency, we only need to compare ourselves to the perfect man, the God-man, Jesus Christ. With little risk of overstatement, we can affirm that He was a man of prayer. His three years of ministry were arguably the busiest, most tedious, and most demanding ever recorded, and yet He excelled as a man of prayer.

It has been said by many that if we read the Gospel of Mark correctly, we will be exhausted after only a few pages. It is arranged like a series of rapid snapshots of Christ as He labors to accomplish His Father's will. Several times in the first chapter, we find the word "immediately" applied to Christ's activities: *immediately* He came up out of the baptismal waters (v. 10); *immediately* the Spirit impelled Him to go out into the wilderness (v. 12); *immediately* He called John and James (v. 20); *immediately* on the Sabbath He entered the synagogue and began to teach (v. 21); *immediately* after they came out of the synagogue, He came into the house of Simon and Andrew (v. 29); and *immediately* they spoke to Him about Simon's sick mother-in-law and He healed her (vv. 30–31). Afterwards on the same day, Mark records: "At evening, when the sun had set, they brought to Him all who were sick and those who were demon-possessed. And the whole city was gathered together at the door. Then He healed many who were sick with various diseases, and cast out many demons; and He did not allow the demons to speak, because they knew Him" (vv. 32–34).

Christ's entire day and evening had been given over to doing His Father's will and meeting the needs of His people. We do not even know whether He found any sleep that evening, but we do know that, "Now in the morning, having risen a long while before daylight, He went out and departed to a solitary place; and there He prayed" (v. 35). It is important to note that this text should *not* be used as a proof text for neglecting sleep or forego- ing the need for rest, but only to demonstrate that Jesus recognized the absolute necessity of prayer.

Christ's devotion to prayer is further confirmed in the Gospel of Luke and its many references to the prayer life of Jesus. He prayed at His baptism (Luke 3:21). He "departed and went into a deserted place" to pray as the crowds searched for Him (4:42). In the midst of intense ministry, He often "withdrew into the wilderness and prayed" (5:15–16). Before choosing His disciples, "He went out to the mountain to pray, and continued all night in prayer to God" (6:12). He had been "alone praying" before He announced His coming death to His disciples (9:18–22).

These references to Christ's prayer life culminate in Luke telling us that after He "was praying in a certain place, when He ceased, that one of His disciples said to Him, 'Lord, teach us to pray'" (Luke 11:1). Imagine that! It is never recorded that the disciples asked Jesus to teach them to walk on water, heal the sick, raise the dead, or even preach, but they did ask this one thing—"Teach us to pray!" Could it be that the most spectacular or astounding thing about Christ was His prayer life? His communion with God was like nothing the disciples had ever wit- nessed in a man and they wanted to know how to pray as He prayed!

Of course, we should seek to conform every aspect of our character and ministry to Christ. But in striving after character and ministry, let us not neglect conformity to Christ's devotional or prayer life. "For in Him dwells all the fullness of the Godhead bodily" (Col. 2:9), and yet He was also a real man, and as a man, He is our example.[1] He drew His direction and strength from the Father through the Holy Spirit in prayer. How much more should we recognize the same need and devote ourselves to prayer!

Learning from Christ

In the matter of learning how to pray and giving content to our prayers there are two extremes. On one extreme, there are those who ignore or neglect the teachings of Scripture and pray according to what is right in their own eyes or according to the various impulses of their emotions. While they may claim guidance from the Holy Spirit, they are often guilty of praying in a manner that contradicts the will of the Spirit as it is revealed in the Scriptures. On the other extreme, there are those who boast of being entirely biblical because their prayer life consists of simply reading scriptural prayers and promises back to God. While this can be an edifying practice in moderation, it is beyond the teaching of Scripture to forbid or discourage extemporaneous prayer that is founded upon and guided by the Scriptures. If we were to eliminate all prayer but the reading of Scripture back to God,

1. In 1 Timothy 2:5, the apostle Paul refers to the divine Son as "the man Christ Jesus." In 1 Corinthians 11:1, he writes, "Imitate me, just as I also imitate Christ."

then we must also eliminate the exposition of the Scriptures in preaching and allow only for the public reading of the biblical text.

In contrast to the above-mentioned extremes, the practice of biblical and devout saints throughout church history has been to renew their minds—to cultivate the mind of Christ—through the study of Scripture. In keeping with this thoroughly biblical regimen, we should study the full counsel of God in the Scriptures, increase our knowledge of the person and works of God, advance in our understanding of who we are before God in Christ, and mature in our discernment of the will and promises of God as they are revealed in the Scriptures. Furthermore, we should give ourselves to the study of the doctrine of prayer and meditate upon the prayers found in the Scriptures, to the degree that we "meditate on these things; give yourself entirely to them" so that our "progress [progress in biblical praying] may be evident to all" (1 Tim. 4:15).

The Scriptures abound with model prayers from which we can learn much, but one stands out above them all. In Luke 11:1, the disciples asked Jesus, "Teach us to pray." In response, Jesus taught them what is known as the Lord's Prayer. As Moses said regarding the burning bush, we must "turn aside and see this great sight" (Ex. 3:3).

Evangelicals have often shied away from using the Lord's Prayer as a model for biblical praying because of its misuse in Roman Catholicism. However, we cannot justify our non-use by someone else's misuse. It is an amazing fact that the one time in Scripture when someone asked

Jesus to teach them how to pray, He directed them to the Lord's Prayer. He said:

> "In this manner, therefore, pray:
> Our Father in heaven,
> Hallowed be Your name.
> Your kingdom come.
> Your will be done
> On earth as it is in heaven.
> Give us this day our daily bread.
> And forgive us our debts,
> as we forgive our debtors.
> And do not lead us into temptation,
> but deliver us from the evil one.
> For Yours is the kingdom and the power
> and the glory forever. Amen." (Matt. 6:9–13)

The first gem that we are given in this prayer is the proper attitude of prayer—a balance between familiarity and reverence. God is our perfectly reconciled and loving Father with whom we can freely converse without fear of condemnation. And yet, we must always remember that our Father is the King of heaven, the Lord of all, and deserving of our greatest reverence. Many Bible teachers have rightly made much of the address, "Abba Father." Paul encouraged the believers in Rome, "For you did not receive the spirit of bondage again to fear, but you received the Spirit of adoption by whom we cry out, 'Abba, Father'" (Rom. 8:15). And again, to the church in Galatia, he wrote, "And because you are sons, God has sent forth the Spirit of His Son into your hearts, crying out, 'Abba, Father!'" (Gal. 4:6). These texts certainly provide us with great encouragements to pray in that they assure us that we have an intimate paternal-filial relationship with God. However, the common teaching that "Abba" is the Aramaic equivalent to the English expression "daddy" is unfounded and harmful. We must understand that in the Middle Eastern context of the first century, *abba* clearly communicated endearment and intimacy but without diminishing in the least the reverence that was appropriate in a father-child relationship. The English term "daddy" is wholly inadequate in that it fails to communicate the reverence required in approaching the Holy One of Israel who said, "By those who come near Me I must be regarded as holy; and before all the people I must be glorified" (Lev. 10:3).

The second gem we discover in this prayer is like a multifaceted diamond; there are three individual petitions that are intricately related to one another. These petitions are to be our controlling passion and should represent the bulk of all our praying. They are to be prayed with regard to the individual Christian, the church at large, and the whole of humanity. In the first petition, "Hallowed be Your name," we are praying that God's name be recognized as separate, distinct, and above all other names and that He be honored as such. For ourselves and for the church, we petition God that we might grow in our estimation of Him and our devotion to Him; that He be held in an entirely separate category in our hearts, above all other loves, and without any competing loyalties. For the unbelieving world we are praying that the gospel might advance so as to remove the spiritual blindness from the nations and give them a new heart that they might esteem the person and will of God above all things.

In the second petition, "Your kingdom come," we are petitioning God that His sovereign and rightful rule might become an increasing reality in us individually and in the church collectively; that we might surrender the entirety of ourselves to Him—heart, soul, mind, and strength; and that He be acknowledged as King of kings in every moment, category, and detail of our lives. For the unbelieving world we are praying that it might cease its warfare against God and acknowledge His right to rule in every person, institution, and endeavor; that every facet of society, government, culture, art, and science acknowledge Him as Lord and applaud His sovereign right to rule.

In the third petition, "Your will be done on earth, as it is in heaven," we are petitioning God that our inward surrender to His Lordship might be manifested in outward and active obedience and service; that we might live before Him on earth as we one day will in heaven. With regard to the unbelieving world, we are praying that the gospel might so advance as to reconcile "all nations, tribes, peoples, and tongues" to God and to bring them into willing and joyful submission to the King of kings and Lord of lords (Rev. 7:9).

These three petitions are a revelation of the heart or passion of Christ, and therefore they are to be the central passion of our lives and at the heart of all our praying. As God's people we have one great concern—that His Name be hallowed, that His kingdom come, and that His will be done—in us, in the church, and throughout the globe. Every other desire or need, no matter how valid, is still secondary. Even the petitions that follow in the Lord's

Prayer must be understood in the context of this one concern. Our petitions for daily sustenance, for power over temptation, and for unity in the church are simply so that we can labor with greater focus and efficiency for the honoring of God's name, the advancement of His kingdom, and the doing of His will. We can be assured that God will honor such praying!

In conjunction with the Lord's Prayer there are also a near-countless number of prayers recorded in the Scriptures regarding sanctification in general, illumination for understanding the Scriptures, and guidance and power for the Christian life. To deal briefly with even a tenth of them would require several volumes. However, they are waiting to be found by you in the Scriptures. All that is required is a willingness that proves itself in diligent study.

Private and Corporate Prayer

There are two important contexts of prayer and both of them are essential in the Christian's growth to maturity. The first is private or secret prayer. This includes personal worship, thanksgiving, communion, and the voicing of every manner of biblical petition. Private prayer is absolutely essential in our study of the Scriptures in that we have a constant need for the Spirit's aid. It is the Spirit of God who illumines us to understand the Scriptures[2] and who strengthens us to obey them.[3] Private prayer and personal communion also guard us against a faith that is

2. 1 Corinthians 2:12; 1 John 2:20, 27; Ephesians 1:15–19
3. Ephesians 3:14–16; Colossians 1:29

wholly cerebral, intellectual, or academic rather than also transforming, relational, and practical. We must always remember that true Christianity is more than authoritative truth revealed through an inspired, inerrant, and infallible book. It is also a personal, transformative, and responsive relationship with the God who is revealed through that book.

Accompanying our private or secret prayer life should be a participation in the public or corporate prayer life of the church. Regarding the physical temple in Jerusalem, Jesus declared, "It is written, 'and my house shall be a house of prayer.'"[4] How much more may this quote from Isaiah be applied to Christ's spiritual temple, the church![5] From the Book of Acts, we learn that the early church was devoted to corporate prayer. Luke records, "They continued steadfastly in the apostles' doctrine and fellowship, in the breaking of bread, and in prayers" (Acts 2:42).

In many churches today, corporate prayer suffers from the same neglect as the public reading of the Scriptures. When it is practiced, it is often little more than a town meeting where news or even gossip is shared for a lengthy period, and then the meeting is adjourned with a few minutes of general prayer. It is also not uncommon for the church's corporate prayer to focus primarily on the physical needs of the congregation while the greater needs of the kingdom as manifested in the Lord's Prayer are entirely overlooked.

---

4. Luke 19:46; Isaiah 56:7
5. 1 Corinthians 3:16–17; 6:19; 2 Corinthians 6:16; Ephesians 2:21

To restore the rightful place of corporate or public prayer in the local congregation, the elders must take the lead. They must not only set aside time for prayer and instruct the congregation on the importance of prayer, but they must also teach the church how to pray biblically and correct the unbiblical attitudes and practices that will surface in the corporate prayer meetings. It should be noted that the restoration of prayer to its rightful place in the congregation will nearly be impossible as long as church leaders (especially in the West) continue to promote church gatherings as events that cater to the carnal whims of the unconverted and entertain the immature. May God raise up elders who, like the apostles of the first century, declare with solemn conviction, "but we will give ourselves continually to prayer and to the ministry of the word" (Acts 6:4) and lead the church to do the same!

Chapter Questions and Reflections

1. What do you think about the following statement? "It has often been said by both ministers and laity, 'I have never known of a dying believer who lamented that they had spent too much time in the Word of God and prayer.'" How can this statement be applied to your own life?

2. What are the two primary reasons why we find prayer so difficult?

3. How did Jesus demonstrate in His life that He was a man of prayer? How should we follow His example?

4. What are the two extremes that we should avoid when learning how to pray biblically? How did the biblical and devout saints throughout church history learn to pray?

5. Why should we consider the Lord's Prayer as essential to our understanding of biblical praying?

6. Explain briefly the significance of each of the phrases in the Lord's Prayer.

7. Describe personal or private prayer and its importance.

8. What place did corporate, public prayer have in the life of the early church? What must be done to restore this practice in the church today?

4

Repentance and Confession

Our spiritual forefathers rarely mentioned repentance and confession separately as means of grace because they were considered as essential elements of prayer. In other words, any talk of prayer as a means of grace would have naturally included repentance and confession. Nevertheless, because there is so much misunderstanding and neglect in the contemporary church with regard to repentance and confession, I feel the need to write on them separately as means of grace.

In contemporary culture and in much of evangelicalism, repentance and confession of sin are often looked upon adversely, or at best as necessary evils. Modern psychology has taught us to protect our egos at all cost, even if we must deny reality or lie to each other and ourselves. To make matters worse, much evangelical preaching seems designed to leave every stone unturned so that the light of the Scriptures never exposes our wrongdoing or makes us uncomfortable. We seem dead set on maintaining the status quo of "I'm OK...You're OK," even though all the evidence points to the contrary. As a result, our conscience is afflicted by a gnawing sense of guilt, our peace is overruled by a deep and abiding sense of estrangement from God, and victory is swallowed up by near-perpetual defeat.

What is the remedy for this frequent malady that besets the Christian? As is often the case, the medicine we need is the very medicine we are most inclined to avoid—repentance and confession! Viewed through the eyes of the world, the carnal, and the uninstructed, repentance and confession are demeaning and destructive. Viewed biblically, they are a gift from God, a means of grace that leads to restoration, peace, and joy.

If we are to walk with Christ with the confidence and joy that He intends, we must turn from the world's ideologies and embrace the cure that is found in the Scriptures. The opposing potions of the world and the Word cannot be mixed and prescribed together, except to the patient's harm. We must reject the remedies of the world that would have us merely cover the festering wound of sin. We must embrace the remedy of the Word that tells us to remove the scab and cleanse the wound.

Repentance

In the New Testament, the word "repent" is most frequently translated from the Greek verb *metanoéo,* which is constructed from the verb *noéo* (to perceive or understand) and the preposition *meta* which denotes change. Repentance, therefore, involves a radical change in one's perception of things or in one's view of reality itself. In the Scriptures, this change of mind is never confined to the intellect, but has an equally radical effect upon the emotions and will.

A Hebrew term that adds to our understanding of repentance is the verb *nacham*. It is derived from a root which reflects the idea of "breathing deeply," communicating the physical display of one's feelings, such as sorrow, regret, or contrition.[1] Thus, biblical repentance not only involves a change of mind regarding sin but also a genuine sorrow for sin.

The slightest true comprehension of our sinfulness and guilt will lead to genuine sorrow, shame, and even a healthy hatred or loathing of our sin and our flesh. Ezra the scribe declared that he was "ashamed and humiliated to lift up" his face to God because of Israel's sins (Ezra 9:5–6). The prophet Jeremiah cried out, "We lie down in our shame, and our reproach covers us. For we have sinned against the Lord our God" (Jer. 3:25). The prophet Ezekiel was even so bold as to declare that when disobedient Israel finally recognized the heinous nature of its sin against the Lord, it would loathe itself in its own sight for all the evil things that it had done (Ezek. 20:43). Finally, writing to the believers in Rome, the apostle Paul noted that they were still ashamed of the things that they had done prior to their conversion (Rom. 6:21). Such talk seems out of place in a world and an evangelical community that are overrun with the psychology of self-esteem. Nevertheless, sorrow, shame, and self-hatred are biblical truths and an essential part of genuine repentance in either Testament.

---

1. *Theological Workbook of the Old Testament*, R. Laird Harris, Gleason L. Archer, Jr., Bruce K. Waltke (Chicago: Moody, 1980), 2:570.

To understand repentance we must consider it from two perspectives—repentance unto salvation at the moment of our conversion and ongoing repentance unto sanctification throughout the full course of the Christian life. At the moment of our conversion, the Holy Spirit regenerated our hearts, illuminated our minds, and exposed our error and sin by a revelation of divine truth. As a result of this divine work, our mind was changed and our view of reality was radically altered—especially with regard to God, self, sin, and the way of salvation. We turned from unbelief and autonomy to faith and submission to the will of God. After conversion, the Holy Spirit continues the work of repentance by continuing to reveal divine truth to us, so that with greater and greater clarity we will see God's character and see ourselves in ever-increasing light. And it is in this light that our sins are exposed and we are brought to repentance and confession. This is what many of the old school theologians and preachers referred to as the "Calvary Road,"[2] and it is the only way to freedom and joy!

To understand how repentance and confession lead to life we must first understand that sin of all kinds is a deadly malady to the Christian life. It pollutes,[3] enslaves,[4]

---

2. The book *The Calvary Road* by Roy Hession (Fort Washington, Pa.: Christian Literature Crusade, 1990) is a wonderful work on the topic of biblical repentance that leads to life, joy, and greater sanctification.

3. "But we are all like an unclean thing, and all our righteousnesses are like filthy rags" (Isa. 64:6). " And you have polluted the land with your harlotries and your wickedness" (Jer. 3:2).

4. "Jesus answered them, 'Most assuredly, I say to you, whoever commits sin is a slave of sin'" (John 8:34). "Do you not know that to

makes miserable, and eventually kills everything it touches.[5] Most of all, it hinders the believer's fellowship with God and usefulness to God. While it is a truth worthy of all acceptance that nothing can separate the believer from the love of God that is in Christ Jesus our Lord (Rom. 8:39), it is equally true that sin hinders earthly communion with God. The psalmist cried out, "If I regard iniquity in my heart, the Lord will not hear" (Ps. 66:18). The prophet Isaiah boldly declared to wayward Israel: "Behold, the Lord's hand is not shortened, that it cannot save; nor His ear heavy, that it cannot hear. But your iniquities have separated you from your God; and your sins have hidden His face from you, so that He will not hear." (Isa. 59:1–2).

A cursory view of the defiling and deadly nature of sin in the believer's life and its effect on our communion with God should prompt us to seek a quick and worthy remedy. It should make us willing to administer that remedy to ourselves over and over again throughout the full course of our lives. That remedy is repentance and it is most effective when we saturate our minds with the Scriptures, have fellowship with a biblical local church, and are determined to deal radically with sin when it is exposed.

First, we become sensitive to our sin and our need of repentance as we saturate our lives in the Word of God.

---

whom you present yourselves slaves to obey, you are that one's slaves whom you obey, whether of sin leading to death, or of obedience leading to righteousness?" (Rom. 6:16).

5. "Then, when desire has conceived, it gives birth to sin; and sin, when it is full-grown, brings forth death" (James 1:15).

As David said, there is a direct connection between the filling of the heart with the Word of God and its ability to flee sin (Ps. 119:11). Here we must acknowledge the absolute essentiality of the Word of God in making the believer increasingly sensitive to sin. Although conviction of sin is the work of the Holy Spirit (John 16:8), the sword or scalpel that the Spirit wields to cut the heart is the Word of God. Again, we must reiterate what was stated earlier. The more we see of God's light through our study of the Word, the more we will see ourselves in that light. As we grow in the Word, sins that were previously hidden are exposed and we learn to see sin as God sees it, to hate it with a holy passion, and to reject it without compromise. The Spirit's work in exposing the hidden sin in our lives may often be very painful, gut-wrenching, and heartbreaking, but it is the sure route to a cure. A person who is unaware of the cancer lying within them may be quite happy in their ignorance, but it is a deadly ignorance that will bring certain death. However, the patient who is made aware of his or her cancer may mourn for a season, but the news that breaks their heart ultimately saves their life.

Second, we become sensitive to our sin and our need of repentance as we live out our Christian lives in fellowship with genuine believers in a visible local church. This is often overlooked and even neglected in this present generation. Nevertheless, it is absolutely essential. God has determined that each believer should grow in the context of godly elders, faithful teachers, and the fellowship of the saints. The Old Testament affirms, "As iron sharpens iron, so a man sharpens the countenance of his friend" (Prov. 27:17). The New Testament is even more explicit. The apostle Paul writes that one of the primary tasks of Christ's ministers is to "Preach the word! Be ready in season and out of season. Convince, rebuke, exhort, with all longsuffering and teaching" (2 Tim. 4:2). This kind of ministry is not limited to Christ's ministers, but extends to the entire congregation. Again, Paul writes to the church in Colossae, "Let the word of Christ dwell in you richly in all wisdom, teaching and admonishing one another in psalms and hymns and spiritual songs" (Col. 3:16). With this the writer of Hebrews concurs: "Let us hold fast the confession of our hope without wavering, for He who promised is faithful. And let us consider one another in order to stir up love and good works, not forsaking the assembling of ourselves together, as is the manner of some, but exhorting one another, and so much the more as you see the Day approaching" (Heb. 10:23–25).

If we hold to the inspiration, inerrancy, and sufficiency of the Scriptures, we cannot entertain for a single moment that we can live the Christian life in its fullness or attain to the maturity that pleases God apart from our consistent and practical participation in a biblical local church. There we will find encouragement to press on, direction in the way that we should walk, correction when we have erred or strayed, and discipline in the event that our hearts have become hard and our necks stiff. If this cannot be found in your church, then your church is simply not biblical!

Third, once sin is exposed by the Spirit through the Word, it must be dealt with severely, radically, and without excuse or delay. Jesus declared to His disciples, "If your right eye causes you to sin, pluck it out and cast it from you; for it is more profitable for you that one of your members perish, than for your whole body to be cast into hell. And if your right hand causes you to sin, cut it off and cast it from you; for it is more profitable for you that one of your members perish, than for your whole body to be cast into hell" (Matt. 5:29–30). This is of course a hyperbole,[6] but it correctly and powerfully communicates how we must deal with our sin once it is revealed—we must renounce it without hesitation, compromise, or excuse. We must execute swift judgment upon it, driving the Word of God through its very heart, and casting it from us with great contempt.

Confession of Sin[7]

It is extremely important to understand that genuine repentance not only involves an inward sorrow of the heart and a genuine turning from sin, but it also includes an open confession that God's opinion of us is true and His verdict is just: *we have sinned!* In other words, biblical repentance always involves an owning up to what we have done.

This truth runs contrary to our contemporary culture. We are a self-excusing and self-justifying people who are never truly at fault, but always victims of some malicious,

6. Hyperbole: An exaggerated statement that is not meant to be taken literally, but is intended to emphasize the importance of the truth being communicated.

7. Some content in this section has been adapted from Paul Washer, *The Gospel Call and True Conversion* (Grand Rapids: Reformation Heritage Books, 2013), 1–21.

often nameless, power beyond our control. We find or invent the cleverest means of attributing our sins to anything or anyone outside of ourselves. We self-righteously point the finger at society, education, upbringing, or circumstance, and are appalled and even angered at the slightest suggestion that guilt should be laid at our feet. Nevertheless, at the moment of conversion, this opinion of the age is radically altered. For the first time in our lives we turn our indicting finger back upon ourselves and honestly own up to the wrong that we have done. Our mouths are shut and we see ourselves as accountable to God (Rom. 3:19). We offer no excuse and seek no avenue of escape except His mercy that is made possible through the vicarious suffering of Christ.

This personal acknowledgement of guilt—this attitude of taking full responsibility for our deeds—will also be accompanied by an honest transparency before God and a heartfelt confession of sin. The word "confess" is translated from the Greek word *homologéo,* which is a compound of the words *homos,* meaning "same," and *logos,* meaning "word." It suggests the idea of *speaking the same thing*—that confession is to verbally agree with God that we have sinned and that our sin is heinous. When such confession is genuine, it is also accompanied by sorrow, brokenness, remorse, and regret. When the Holy Spirit through the Word or the rebuke of another tells us that we have sinned, we must speak the same thing back to God in confession. For example, if we have been shown to be self-centered, impatient, and unloving, then we would confess, "Lord, what You say about me is true. I have been self-centered, impatient, and unloving. Please forgive for the sake of Your great name and on the basis of Your Son's atonement."

Notice three essential elements of biblical confession. First, the one confessing does not say, "If I have sinned," or speak of sin in general, but confesses specific sins that have been revealed to him or her by the Holy Spirit according to God's infallible Word.[8] Second, genuine confession offers no excuse, nor does it attempt to transfer blame to another, but it accepts full responsibility for the sin or sins that have been committed. Third, the hope of forgiveness is not founded upon the believer's stored up merits from past good deeds, but solely upon the vicarious sacrifice of Jesus Christ. The mature believer recognizes that his or her only ground for expecting forgiveness from God is "that Christ died for our sins according to the Scriptures, and that He was buried, and that He rose again the third day according to the Scriptures" (1 Cor. 15:3–4).

There is a fourth essential element of confession that is not explicit in the above prayer that must be marked and emphasized, for without it repentance is nonsensical and useless. This is faith. We must believe the promises of God that offer forgiveness and cleansing for even the greatest sins of the broken and contrite. One of the most difficult things for even the most mature believer to do is to comprehend the magnitude of God's forgiveness. When rightly understood, His grace will seem too good to be true—even wrong! And it would be, if not for the

8. It is important to note that the subjective convicting work of the Holy Spirit will always be in agreement with the sound doctrine of the written Word.

cross of our Lord and Savior Jesus Christ, who paid sin's debt to the satisfaction of divine justice and the appeasement of divine wrath. Apart from a correct view of the cross, we will be prone like Peter to cry out in the midst of our sin, "Depart from me, for I am a sinful man, O Lord!" (Luke 5:8). But one true look at Calvary will prove to the most fragile heart that a fountain has been opened for sin and for uncleanness (Zech. 13:1). And it will embolden that fragile heart to cry out, "Pardon the iniquity of this people, I pray, according to the greatness of Your mercy" (Num. 14:19).

We must hold firmly to the promises of God because we are too prone to think that He is somehow like us (Ps. 50:21), and that His mercy, grace, and forgiveness bear the same limits and restrictions as ours. We must always remember that "For as the heavens are higher than the earth, so are My ways higher than your ways, and My thoughts than your thoughts" (Isa. 55:9). We think of ourselves as magnanimous because we boast of extending forgiveness up to seven times, and we forget that God's grace is still not spent at seventy times seven.[9] We are also hindered from comprehending and availing ourselves of God's forgiveness because of the devil's accusations against us, his slander of God's character, his depreciation of the efficaciousness of the cross, and his denial of the unconditional nature of grace. If the devil cannot downplay our sin so that we see no need of

---

9. "Then Peter came to Him, and said, 'Lord, how often shall my brother sin against me, and I forgive him? Up to seven times?' Jesus said to him, 'I do not say to you, up to seven times, but up to seventy times seven'" (Matt. 18:21–22).

repentance, then he will magnify our sin so as to make us believe that though forgiveness is needed, it cannot be obtained, and that we have run beyond the boundaries of divine grace and into the realm of hopelessness. If this cannot be achieved, the devil will at least seek to make us doubt God's goodness and convince us to draw away from Him until a proper period of time when God's wrath has subsided and we have proven the sincerity of our brokenness. The lies of the devil are strong and have taken down greater saints than you and me. The only shield or bulwark against his flaming arrow is holding fast to the promises of God. A good rule of thumb in this warfare of ours is this: although God may expose our sin with a terrible frankness and a painful rebuke, He will always end the matter with the exhortation that we run to Him and not from Him. Any voice that sends the sinful believer away from God is of the flesh, the world, and the devil. It is not from God! It is the testimony of Scripture that godly sorrow for sin is highly esteemed by Him:

> The sacrifices of God are a broken spirit, a broken and a contrite heart—These, O God, You will not despise. (Ps. 51:17)

> For thus says the High and Lofty One who inhabits eternity, whose name is Holy: "I dwell in the high and holy place, with him who has a contrite and humble spirit, to revive the spirit of the humble, and to revive the heart of the contrite ones. (Isa. 57:15)

> But on this one will I look: On him who is poor and of a contrite spirit, and who trembles at My word. (Isa. 66:2)

> Blessed are those who mourn, for they shall be comforted. (Matt. 5:4)

> Blessed are those who hunger and thirst for righteousness, for they shall be filled. (Matt. 5:6)

It is this kindness and willingness of God to forgive that makes genuine repentance and confession a means of grace and a cause for great joy. As believers, we should not neglect the Word or close our ears to the Spirit when sin is exposed in us. Rather, we should humble ourselves, acknowledge our sin, turn from it, and run to the throne room of God, the doors of which have been forever thrown open wide by the blood of Jesus Christ. The writer of Hebrews explains and exhorts: "For we do not have a High Priest who cannot sympathize with our weaknesses, but was in all points tempted as we are, yet without sin. Let us therefore come boldly to the throne of grace, that we may obtain mercy and find grace to help in time of need" (Heb. 4:15–16).

The Marks of Faith

Before we advance any further, it is important to note that sensitivity to sin, repentance, and confession are not merely the marks of Christian maturity, but the hallmarks of genuine conversion. Even the most recent converts will demonstrate a new and adverse disposition toward sin and will practice repentance and confession. Conversely, the lack of repentance and confession may be evidence that a person is still in an unconverted state. Regarding this matter, the apostle John wrote, "If we say that we have no sin, we deceive ourselves, and the truth is not in us [that is, we are not Christian]. If we confess our sins, He is faithful and just to forgive us our sins and to cleanse us from all unrighteousness [that is, we are Christian]. If we say that we have not sinned, we make Him a liar, and His word is not in us [that is, we are not Christian]" (1 John 1:8–10).[10]

One of the greatest evidences of true conversion is not sinless perfection, as some have erroneously supposed. Instead, it is a sensitivity to sin, a renouncing of sin, an open confession of sin, and the joy of forgiveness. For this reason, genuine believers will appear as something of a paradox to outsiders. On one hand, they may be described as "those who mourn" (Matt. 5:4), but on the other hand, they are marked by "joy inexpressible and full of glory" (1 Peter 1:8).

As believers grow in their knowledge of the character and will of God, they begin to see their sin and lack of conformity to God in a greater light. This leads them to a more profound brokenness or mourning over sin. Thus, they may properly be identified as "those who mourn." At the same time, as they grow in their knowledge of God, they also behold more of His mercy and grace in the person and redemptive work of Christ. This leads them to a more profound joy in the God of their salvation. Thus, with each passing year their mourning and their joy increase hand in hand until the end of their days when

10. The statements in brackets are mine.

they will be found utterly broken and yet filled with "joy inexpressible and full of glory." When asked how such a mixture of mourning and joy might be found in the same person, they reply, "I am a great sinner, but Christ is a greater Savior." Also, take note of the great transition. Their joy is no longer found in their tarnished virtue or mutable performance, but in the cross of Christ and the grace of God that flows from it!

The Joy of Application

Having learned these important truths, we must now examine our lives and our Christian profession in light of them. Are we growing in our knowledge of God's holiness and in turn becoming more and more sensitive to the sin in our own lives? Do we react to our sin with a greater sense of repugnance and disdain? Do we battle against it? Does the weight of our sin coupled with the kindness of God lead us to repentance and confession (Rom. 2:4)? If we have answered in the affirmative, there is evidence that God has done something of a saving work in us, but there is need to persevere and to grow. Let us always be of the mindset to "search out and examine our ways, and turn back to the Lord" (Lam. 3:40). If God were a harsh and unloving deity who condemned without mercy, then we would be right to do everything in our power to hide our sin or outright deny it. But our God is "merciful and gracious, slow to anger, and abounding in mercy" (Ps. 103:8). He has sent His only Son to pay for every one of our transgressions from the first to the last. The Scriptures prove that He has "no pleasure in the death of the wicked, but that the wicked turn from his way and live"

(Ezek. 33:11). Therefore, let us turn from our evil ways and live. The Scriptures argue that wrath is God's "awesome work,"[11] but He longs to be gracious and He waits on high to show compassion (Isa. 30:18). Because of these truths regarding the character of God, we must never view repentance and confession as executioners leading us to condemnation and death, but as handmaidens of our God that lead us to Christ's blood which washes us white as snow and returns us to His presence.

Chapter Questions and Reflections

1. Write a biblical definition of repentance. Incorporate into your definition the meaning of the Greek verb *metanoéō* and the Hebrew verb *nacham*.

2. Sin is a great malady in the Christian life. Explain how unconfessed sin is a detriment to the believer's life.

3. How is genuine repentance dependent upon our knowledge of the Scriptures?

11. "For the Lord will rise up as at Mount Perazim, He will be angry as in the Valley of Gibeon—that He may do His work, His awesome work, and bring to pass His act, His unusual act" (Isa. 28:21).

4. How is genuine repentance dependent upon our fellowship with other believers in the context of a local church?

5. How should the Christian react to sin or deal with sin once it is exposed?

6. Write a biblical definition of the word "confession." Incorporate into your definition the meaning of the Greek verb *homologéō.*

7. What are the four essential elements of biblical confession?

8. Why is it so important to grow in our knowledge of God's promises regarding forgiveness and to hold tenaciously to those promises?

9. Why should the discovery of sin cause the Christian to run toward God in hope rather than away from Him in fear?

10. Why does the devil seek to cause God's people to doubt God's forgiveness? What can we do to withstand him?

11. What is God's disposition to the believer who is broken over his or her sin and seeking forgiveness? What are some of the most important Scriptures regarding this matter?

12. Explain how the Christian can be described as both mourning and joyful.

13. Explain how repentance and confession are a gift from God, a means of grace that leads to restoration, peace, and joy.

14. Explain the following statement: "Because of the gracious character of God, we must never view repentance and confession as executioners leading us to condemnation and death, but as handmaidens of our God that lead us to Christ's blood which washes us white as snow and returns us to His presence."

5

The Church

Having briefly considered the Scriptures and prayer as a means of grace, we will now turn to the church, its fellowship, and its ordinances. From the outset, it is necessary that we define our terms to ensure that we are on the same page. In this chapter, the term "church" is used with reference to a local visible body of believers, committed to one another, shepherded by elder-qualified men,[1] served by biblically qualified deacons,[2] devoted to biblical exposition and prayer, holding to the ordinances, and practicing church discipline. A local church is not synonymous with a weekly Bible study, a *parachurch* ministry, or listening to one's favorite preachers on the internet. This distinction is important because many believe that they are obeying the command to congregate through informal fellowships which may be helpful but are no substitute for God's non-negotiable plan of fellowship in a biblical local church.

The road to greater Christian maturity and usefulness is a difficult one. However, difficulty becomes near

1. 1 Timothy 3:1–7; Titus 1:5–9
2. 1 Timothy 3:8–13

impossibility when we seek to grow and persevere in the faith outside of the context of a visible local church and a real relationship with teaching and ruling elders who teach, shepherd, and lead. For this reason, it is not merely helpful, but absolutely essential that we work out our salvation in the context of a local church and its elders who know our name and watch over our lives. For this reason, the writer of Hebrews warns: "Let us hold fast the confession of our hope without wavering, for He who promised is faithful. And let us consider one another in order to stir up love and good works, not forsaking the assembling of ourselves together, as is the manner of some, but exhorting one another, and so much the more as you see the Day approaching" (Heb. 10:23–25).

Today there is cause for lamenting a dearth of biblical churches as described above—shepherded by elder-qualified men, served by biblically qualified deacons, devoted to biblical exposition and prayer, holding to the ordinances, and practicing church discipline. However, we must also take care that we do not become judgmental and severe and demand that a church be perfect corporately while we remain imperfect as individuals. A momentary glimpse of ourselves in the mirror of God's Word will reveal a long series of imperfections and a lengthy "to do" list. For this reason and many others, we should be careful that we do not demand from the church what we ourselves have failed to achieve in our own personal lives. We should not demand a perfect church, but rather we should seek for one whose elders and congregation are growing in their knowledge of God's standard and striving toward that mark.

Elder-Qualified Shepherds

One of the greatest means of grace that God has given us is faithful and humble ministers of the gospel who bear the biblical qualifications of an elder[3] and are devoted to prayer and the ministry of the Word (Acts 6:2, 4). This truth is set forth with amazing clarity in the apostle Paul's letter to the church in Ephesus: "And He Himself gave some to be apostles, some prophets, some evangelists, and some pastors and teachers, for the equipping of the saints for the work of ministry, for the edifying of the body of Christ, till we all come to the unity of the faith and of the knowledge of the Son of God, to a perfect man, to the measure of the stature of the fullness of Christ" (Eph. 4:11–13). This text proves beyond a shadow of a doubt that it is Christ Himself who gives faithful ministers to the church for its edification. Will we neglect or even despise these gifts? Will we depreciate their significance? Will we act as if we do not need the very medicine that Christ has prescribed?

A sincere but misguided believer might respond to the above questions, saying, "But there are no ministers who are elder-qualified and faithful to their calling as prescribed by the Scriptures." The answer to this objection is two-fold. First, to say that there are no faithful ministers of Christ on the earth is not so much a critique of the ministers as it is a denial of the sovereignty and power of Christ! This is Christ's church and He is its supplier and support. It is true that there are many charlatans and usurpers, but Christ will always have His "seven

3. 1 Timothy 3:1–7; Titus 1:6–9

thousand men who have not bowed the knee to Baal" (Rom. 11:4; 1 Kings 19:18). Second, we must realize that even the best of men will never match the perfection of Christ as they minister on this side of glory. Therefore, even though we may expect that elders meet the biblical qualifications of their office and that they perform their duty with faithfulness, we must not demand from any man more than is prescribed by the Scriptures. Even the great apostle Paul wrote of himself, "Not that I have already attained, or am already perfected; but I press on, that I may lay hold of that for which Christ Jesus has also laid hold of me. Brethren, I do not count myself to have apprehended; but one thing I do, forgetting those things which are behind and reaching forward to those things which are ahead, I press toward the goal for the prize of the upward call of God in Christ Jesus" (Phil. 3:12–14).

Having given the above caution to the layperson, let me now give the following instruction and warning to ministers. All ministers have been called to biblical faithfulness and all will be judged accordingly. We must not take the mantle of ministry upon ourselves or allow others to recruit us into the ministry unless in good conscience we meet the qualifications set forth in the Scriptures[4] and a mature congregation is able to affirm these specific qualifications in our character and behavior. These qualifications are not options or something to "grow into" later, but they are non-negotiable demands. Furthermore, we must acknowledge that our ministries are to be designed and confined by what is written in the Scriptures. We are

4. 1 Timothy 3:1–7; Titus 1:6–9

not given the freedom to write our own job description or script. We must be utterly convinced that the requirements and duties of the ministry are clearly revealed in the Scriptures and that we are called to submit to them fearfully and wholeheartedly. The mantle of ministry is both a privilege and a grave responsibility. If we are ministers of Christ, let the following warnings find their way into the deepest recesses of our hearts and minds, even to the deepest marrow of our bones:

> Now if anyone builds on this foundation with gold, silver, precious stones, wood, hay, straw, each one's work will become clear; for the Day will declare it, because it will be revealed by fire; and the fire will test each one's work, of what sort it is. If anyone's work which he has built on it endures, he will receive a reward. If anyone's work is burned, he will suffer loss; but he himself will be saved, yet so as through fire. (1 Cor. 3:12–15)

> Therefore we make it our aim, whether present or absent, to be well pleasing to Him. For we must all appear before the judgment seat of Christ, that each one may receive the things done in the body, according to what he has done, whether good or bad. (2 Cor. 5:9–10)

> My brethren, let not many of you become teachers, knowing that we shall receive a stricter judgment. (James 3:1)

No matter how mature a Christian believes himself or herself to be or how many years they have been in the faith, they need to be under the teaching and shepherding of godly and humble elders. This is not my private opinion regarding some optional strategy of ministry, but it is Christ's plan for His church. You and I do not need eloquent speakers, powerful personalities, detached celebrity preachers, spiritual dictators, or greedy men who feed upon the flock. However, we do need good shepherds who lay down their lives for the sheep[5] and faithful and sensible stewards who give God's people their proper rations.[6]

Communion of the Saints

Another means of grace within the context of the local church is the ministry of the saints. Paul's letter to the Ephesians makes it clear that ministers have not been given to the church to do all the ministry, but "for the equipping of the saints for the work of ministry, for the edifying of the body of Christ" (Eph. 4:12). The Holy Spirit has especially gifted every member of the local church in order that each might contribute to the ministry of that local church. Subsequently, this also proves that every member of the church has need of the rest of the body. There are no "lone wolves" in a biblically mature Christianity. In fact, Hebrews 10:23–25 (quoted above) warns us not to forsake the assembling of ourselves together because we have a great need to be stimulated and encouraged by the other members of the congregation.

5. "I am the good shepherd. The good shepherd gives His life for the sheep" (John 10:11).

6. "And the Lord said, 'Who then is that faithful and wise steward, whom his master will make ruler over his household, to give them their portion of food in due season?'" (Luke 12:42).

This is a constant theme throughout the entire New Testament. Here is a brief sample:

> There are diversities of gifts, but the same Spirit. There are differences of ministries, but the same Lord. And there are diversities of activities, but it is the same God who works all in all. But the manifestation of the Spirit is given to each one for the profit of all. (1 Cor. 12:4–7)

> As each one has received a gift, minister it to one another, as good stewards of the manifold grace of God. (1 Peter 4:10)

> Let the word of Christ dwell in you richly in all wisdom, teaching and admonishing one another in psalms and hymns and spiritual songs, singing with grace in your hearts to the Lord. (Col. 3:16)

Dear brothers and sisters, our need of a local body cannot be exaggerated. It is in the context of a local church that we are called to give and receive ministry for the edification of all. Not even the great apostle Paul was beyond the need of this wonderful means of grace. To the church in Rome he wrote: "For I long to see you, that I may impart to you some spiritual gift, so that you may be established—that is, that I may be encouraged together with you by the mutual faith both of you and me" (Rom. 1:11–12).

The Ordinances

In the New Testament church there are two ordinances—baptism and the Lord's Supper. Throughout history many evangelicals have preferred to use the term "ordinance" rather than "sacrament" in order to avoid any possibility that their language might communicate the erroneous belief that salvation is in anyway conferred through baptism or the Lord's Supper. The doctrine of baptismal regeneration and the belief that Christ is corporally present in the bread and wine are grave errors. The Lord's Supper is a memorial to Christ's death and resurrection and is to be practiced in remembrance of Him and as a proclamation, sign, and seal of His redemptive work on behalf of the church (1 Cor. 11:23–26). Baptism is a public declaration of the believer's faith in Christ and a public identification with His person, His gospel, and His people. Although we must denounce the slightest inclination to believe that baptism and the Lord's Supper are means of saving grace, we should seek to promote their great significance and usefulness as means of sanctifying grace in a manner similar to the reading and preaching of the Scriptures and congregational prayer. In both ordinances, Christ is proclaimed and is also present with His people. After His discourse on church discipline, Christ declared, "For where two or three are gathered together in My name, I am there in the midst of them" (Matt. 18:20). If such a promise is applicable to the church when it is gathered to pronounce discipline on an unrepentant member, how much more does it apply to the gathering of the local church for baptism and the Lord's Supper?

The importance of the ordinances of baptism and the Lord's Supper can hardly be exaggerated. However, in the evangelical church's rightful attempt to avoid portraying these ordinances as means of salvation, we have often portrayed them with less significance, dignity, and solemnity than they deserve. Elders must not only teach on the biblical view of these two ordinances, but they must also communicate to the congregation their special significance and instruct believers how to prepare their hearts and minds for such.

Church Discipline

In the minds of many, the mere mention of church discipline evokes images of legalism, self-righteousness, hypocrisy, lovelessness, and cruelty. Oftentimes, it is rebutted with other Scriptures taken out of context: "Judge not, that you be not judged" (Matt. 7:1) or "He who is without sin among you, let him throw a stone at her first" (John 8:7). These negative opinions and rebuttals can often be traced to three distinct sources—past instances in which church discipline has been practiced in an unbiblical manner, a blatant ignorance of the Scriptures, or anti-biblical, carnal, and worldly opinions regarding what it means truly to love and demonstrate spiritual concern for another.

We must never forget that Jesus commanded that local congregations practice church discipline (Matt. 18:15–17). Although unbiblical practices of church discipline must be strongly rejected and rebuked, we cannot throw out the baby with the bathwater. It was commanded by the Lord of love as a means of protecting, purifying, and leading His church to greater maturity. To reject the practice of church discipline or to accept it in theory while neglecting its practice is a rejection of the Lord Himself and His sovereign reign over the church. Furthermore, it will result in untold damage to the congregation and hinder its progress in maturity.

Having affirmed the validity of church discipline, we must ask how church discipline promotes spiritual maturity in the congregation. To begin, we must first understand that church discipline begins long before any decision to expel a member even comes into view. Church discipline begins with receiving new members and doing due diligence to ensure that they truly understand the gospel and have a good hope that they have been converted. Second, church discipline is also manifested in the diligent exposition of the Scriptures and in the elders' personal shepherding of the members of the congregation. Third, when a member actually falls into sin, the first stage of discipline involves private instruction and correction. If there is no sign of repentance, then one or two other mature Christians (preferably elders) are asked to participate in order to discern and offer counsel. Finally, if there is still no repentance the matter is brought before the church (Matt. 18:15–17). Only as a last result is the member excommunicated from the church. But even then, if the erring member repents, he or she is received back into the congregation with love and forgiveness.[7]

To bring this chapter to a fitting conclusion, we must reiterate that real and active membership in a local church is absolutely essential to the Christian's growth to spiritual maturity. God has given us the local congregation

---

7. A few important biblical texts for church discipline are found in Matthew 18:15–20; 1 Corinthians 5:1–6:11; 2 Corinthians 2:1–11; Romans 16:17; Galatians 6:1; 2 Thessalonians 3:6; Titus 3:10; Jude 22–23.

and its elder-shepherds to aid us in an often long and difficult journey. As is evident from the Scriptures, it is a dangerous journey that is not to be made alone. We should submit to God's will and become a vital member of a local church that demonstrates a sincere pursuit of Christ and His commands as they are revealed in the Scriptures.

Chapter Questions and Reflections

1. How is "church" defined in this chapter? Why is it important to define church in this way?

2. Explain the following statement: "We should be careful that we do not demand from a church what we ourselves have failed to achieve in our own personal lives. We should not demand a perfect church, but rather we should seek for one whose elders and congregation are growing in their knowledge of God's standard and striving toward the mark."

3. Explain the following statement: "One of the greatest means of grace that God has given us is faithful and humble ministers of the gospel who bear the biblical qualifications of an elder and are devoted to prayer and the ministry of the word."

4. Why is it important to recognize that the qualifications of an elder set forth in 1 Timothy 3:1–7 and Titus 1:6–9 are not options or something to "grow into" later, but are non-negotiable demands?

5. Explain the following assertion: "You and I do not need eloquent speakers, powerful personalities, detached celebrity preachers, spiritual dictators, or greedy men who feed upon the flock. However, we do need good shepherds who lay down their lives for the sheep[8] and faithful and sensible stewards who give God's people their rations."

5. In light of Ephesians 4:12 and Colossians 3:16, explain how the communion of the saints in the local church is a means of grace.

6. Explain the meaning of this affirmation: "There are no 'lone wolves' in a biblically mature Christianity."

7. Explain the meaning and purpose of baptism and the Lord's Supper. How can they rightly be called a means of grace?

---

8. "I am the good shepherd. The good shepherd gives His life for the sheep" (John 10:11).

8. Explain the following statement: "Although we must denounce the slightest inclination to believe that baptism and the Lord's Supper are means of saving grace, we should seek to promote their great significance and usefulness as means of sanctifying grace."

9. Who is the author of church discipline? How does this prove that church discipline is a biblical means of grace through which God's people can be protected, corrected, and edified? How does this prove that biblical church discipline is a genuine manifestation of love toward the offending and unrepentant member?

6

In Defense of Simplicity

We have come to the end of this short book introducing the means of grace for growth in sanctification—Scripture, prayer, repentance and confession, and the ministry of the local church. However, before we conclude, I must address the frequent objection that what I have written is overly simplistic—that the Christian's weaknesses and maladies are far too varied and complex to be healed or overcome by such a simple remedy. To this objection I will offer only three comments.

First, the common difficulties in the Christian life,[1] although complex, flow from only a few fountains—the flesh, the world, and the devil. Though we are new creatures in Christ and our identity is no longer determined by our past relationship with Adam (2 Cor. 5:17), there remains within every believer a remnant of our fallen

1. Here I want to make it clear that I am referring to the *typical* difficulties or obstacles to sanctification that are common to all believers. I am not addressing extraordinary cases of individuals who are suffering from extreme mental or emotional disorders, etc. Although they will greatly benefit from the "normal" means of grace they may also require the aid of competent medical professionals, biblical counselors, etc.

humanity, or flesh, that lusts or wars against the Spirit. To the church in Galatians Paul writes, " For the flesh lusts against the Spirit, and the Spirit against the flesh; and these are contrary to one another, so that you do not do the things that you wish. But if you are led by the Spirit, you are not under the law" (Gal. 5:17–18).

Without a doubt the believer's greatest battle is with the flesh, for even the world and the devil are only able to draw, sway, and tempt us because of the lusts of the flesh. As James writes, "But each one is tempted when he is drawn away by his own desires and enticed" (James 1:14). Thus, to overcome the flesh and its lusts is to win the battle. And this spiritual battle is most effectively won through the means of grace that we have set forth—Scripture, prayer, and the ministry of the local church.

Second, although I may have offered a simple solution and armed you with but few weapons to fight this war, the Scriptures validate what I have offered. It is your choice if you wish to draw medicine from another dispensary or weapons from another armory. However, the thoughts and strategies of men are vanity and the flesh avails nothing (John 6:63). Only those weapons that are given to us in the Scriptures are "mighty in God for pulling down strongholds, casting down arguments and every high thing that exalts itself against the knowledge of God, bringing every thought into captivity to the obedience of Christ" (2 Cor. 10:4–5).

Third, I find that those who doubt the power of the means of grace are often neglectful in taking full advantage of them. At the risk of redundancy, I must return to the questions that I asked in a previous chapter: Have we really learned all that the Scriptures have to tell? Have we emptied all of God's promises in prayer? Does our intimacy with the Father, Son, and Holy Spirit have no more room to grow? Have we reaped every benefit that is to be gained from fellowship with a local church? Or is it not more likely that we have been derelict or at least careless, even slothful, with these ordinary but essential means of grace? When someone raises an eyebrow regarding the efficacy of the means of grace that I have set forth, I ask them how much time they spend in the Word, in prayer, and in fellowship with the elders and congregation of a biblical local church. Most bow their heads, shrug their shoulders, and admit their neglect. I have yet to meet a soul so brazen as to say they have exhausted these means to no effect.

Dear brothers and sisters, let us pray believingly and persistently for revival, but until it comes, let us devote ourselves to these ordinary means of grace through which we may become quite extraordinary in conformity and usefulness to Christ.

Your brother,
Paul David Washer